Wild Roses

L. G. Mason

American Literary Press
Baltimore, Maryland

Wild Roses

Copyright © 2005 L. G. Mason

Library of Congress
Cataloging-in-Publication Data
ISBN 1-56167-911-9

Library of Congress Card Catalog Number:
2005904866

Published by

American Literary Press
8019 Belair Road, Suite 10
Baltimore, Maryland 21236

Manufactured in the United States of America

For Adrienne

Acknowledgements

"In November" and "Wild Roses" first appeared in *Thema*. "November Flight," "Class Act," and "Cardiac" were first published in *The Lyric*.

Contents

The Crazy Sacred Flowing of the Year

Saints

Love Stories

Consecration of the House

Each Other We Have Not Always

The Silences God Sings While Fishes Dance

The Crazy Sacred Flowing
of the Year

Class Act

Butterfly, unspin
your springwound song
above the nectar.
Trip astairewise
off a petal,
treading, light and drunken,
on the crazy stairways
of the dawn.

Dragonfly Nymphs

Do they (prowling in the bottom
in prophetic autumn,
in the unforgiving winter)
dream of wings? Do they know
the air is theirs?
Even as the water over them,
beginning at the shores
is turning brittle,
surface growing still
and deepening to stone,
the world going dark
beneath the snow,
do they know? Forget it.
Murders to commit,
better things to do than dream.
Oh, but Lord,
imagine the observances,
if dragonflies were men:
the reveling
in their deliverance,
the glory in the vision
of the parting of the water
and the freeing of the chosen
to the sky.

Egypt

Locusts

Out of a black horizon
at morning,
whisper of wings
on a desert air
turning to thunder.
Voiceless breath
of the gods gone mad.
Come to dismember
the grain
over the river.
Only the falcon (his eye
writ on the wing
of the locust)
can rescue the sky.

The Crocodile Prince

Carried Isis-gentle
to his kingdom on the Nile,
staring wide-eyed
out the windows
of his Mama's smile.

Ibises

Some one long ago
saw at dawn the holy birds
scribbling with their styluses
among the reeds
along the River Nile.
Some one saw at dusk
a line of them against a moon
the color of papyrus.

The Scarab

Falling through grain
into the cattle
and out of the cattle, the Sun
cried out to the beetle,
who molding him
into the shape of a sun again,
wheelbarrowed him home
to the horizon.

Great Blue Heron

In the mist,
in the twilight calm,
the silhouette in the nest
high in the willows
over the lake.
Slender, tranquil her face,
poised over the elegant
curve of the neck.
The vision gives way at dawn
to the heron treading
in shallows,
probing in shallows.
Elegance now is a weapon
for striking at fishes,
arc of her neck a device
to deliver under the surface
a spear of a face.
And kill
whomever she needs to kill
to keep elegance whole.

Tarantula

Drawing herself
out of herself,
slipping the skin,
confessing the twin,
the elegant
black-velvet clone.
Surfacing new,
innocent,
if for only a minute
of everything she
and I and you
and everything deadly
needs to commit.

Jazzman

This cat he hassle
a mouse of a tune
til he get it
as crazy as he is.
This cat he chase it
into a place it
ain' never been.
Up tempo and down,
in this key and that one.
This cat he do
a old song all new,
all different and true
and reborn
on a ride through
a horn.

Caterpillars Dancing

Stepping to the gypsy rhythm
on a city lawn.
Bristling with gypsy-edges
flashing in the sun.
Strutting home
in twilight to the hedges
and the trees, and stripping
summer to the bone.
Where's it written
God meant men
to waste the world alone?

April

Here a stem
beneath a stone rehearses,
there a bit of fur stirs,
here a pair of feelers,
half-a-dozen feet
cannot help tapping.
Nobody can tell
when it will begin,
the tune, but no one
can be still
who knows the beat.

The Forsaken

Plummeting out of the sky,
the wild geese,
into the fenced-in pond at the park.
One of them missing the mark,
plodding round the perimeter,
walking with us in circles
while the season assembles
again on the water.
One of the company
peering as we do from somewhere-
out-of-the-pilgrimage
in at the year.

In the Land of the Giants
(A Fairy Tale)

The giants year after year
thrust the rough of their bodies
up through the vapor, and any time
one of them fell, somebody dwelt there,
somebody hewed out a place
for her young
in the sweet rotting fiber.
And the princess wings lay
deep in the chambers,
deep in the hollows cut in a fallen giant,
pressed one to another
awaiting the festival of the sky.
And they rose up in their magical hour
into the branches of giants,
among whose leaves
the dragons waited. And trolls,
spinning exquisite deadly snares
to murder them in. And many were slain.
But one flew in a lover's embrace:
one high over the vapor
found a prince in the very
breath of the sun,
and coming home to a fallen giant,
surrendered her wings
and dwelt in the wood with her children
til heaven would have them.

Riverdance

If water flows, and nothing in it
lies in wait to mate and murder,
it is only water.
But if eyes in it discover one another,
and if dancers hover
in the air above it,
and if wings in the pursuit of wings
scatter all the makings
of a season on it,
then it is a river.
Then it is the crazy sacred
flowing of the year.

November Flight

In the mad time,
find the way
to make the sky rhyme:
steal the season
from the storm,
endow the day
with (in lieu of reason)
form.

Saints

A Love Story

In the years of the delirium,
when Black Plague hung
in every corridor,
Jesus came into
the dreaming of a young girl,
and she cherished him
as she had never loved before.
As a token of her love,
and as a sign
to other boys who
might have wanted her,
she cut off all her golden hair.

There is a story that her father
(though he long had trusted
she would marry money)
gave her up to Jesus
when one luminescent morning
he beheld a dove
hovering about her as she prayed.

Jesus and a young girl
in one of their finer dreams
were betrothed.
She had his ring,
though in her lifetime,
no one could see it but her.
On one of their nights together,
Jesus revealed to her
He (not she) was the dreamer,
she was the dream.

When she told the people,
they took it for miracle.
People found in anyone's dream
what they could, in a time
of plague. People came
from every corner of creation
just to hear her counsel,
just to touch her hand.
She even (on a roll)
told His Holiness
(languishing in Avignon)
"Get thee for the love of Christ
to Rome, and be a *real* Pope."
And He went.

And when she died,
the ring she had from Jesus
stood out on her hand,
a sign to all the people:
In the shadow of the plague,
salvation is to be
alive and mad
and still in love with God,
no matter what.

Saul

Full of the righteous
fury and glory of God,
I rode to Damascus.
Pricked on the way
by the usual thorn,
an accustomed madness
spreading over my body.
Covered in sweat
and deadly-pale (they say)
I rode to Damascus.

Then all the light in creation
fell over me, every
aura, voice, and sun
celebrated my
flesh and my senses.
All the words in the world
became One Word.
Hell and the heavens opened,
striking me down
with the glory
and grace of infirmity.
And I heard
as I fell, "Saul,
why are you persecuting me?"

And the thorn
that spurred me to grace
has turned to quill
and grown to fledgling in my hand.
It journeys to the gentiles
with the news of son and father
over all the miles,
over all (God willing)
the millennia
til Christ's return.

For This is My Body

At the altar one Sunday,
delirious at her tryst with the Lord,
kneeling, her eyes closed,
her lips parted. How gently
the handsome young priest
(as she opened)
laid the unleavened life in her.
And she wanted to sing,
but bowing her head,
she only rose and departed.
And with a Madonna-like grace,
bore the son of God
to her place.

Saint Rose of the Mosquitoes

Like angelsong,
the humming at the onset
of a summernight.
You running to the window
let your robes slip off,
stood arms spread to heaven,
waiting to be
violated by your Lord,
to share your blood
with all his brethren, bear
the mark of his unmerciful
redeeming sky.

Deliverance

Aunt May,
to save an infant from the Devil,
carried her away
one weekend to be
baptized in the Catholic faith.
Her co-conspirator,
the cloak-and-dagger father,
rigged a secret ceremony
and the child was Catholic evermore.
Though to watch her lead her life,
you never would have known
she had been saved.
Not until she (lapsing
into last days)
chose a final book:
Catholic paperback apology
she carried with her everywhere,
the pages of it
like the layers of her mind
pealing one by one away,
til she belonged again
to God or nobody.

Caterpillar Song

My mother
shared with woolly bears
a corpulent design,
a taste for flagrant colors,
and a yen for dandelion.
Used to gather
off the lawn as they did
fixings for a salad.
Shared with them as well
a fetish for the metamorphic,
lining all tomorrow
with an other-worldly sheen,
spinning, out of elements
of Catholic bric-a-brac,
a sturdy thread,
weaving a cocoon
of (not silk) prayer,
of preparation for some
world to come.

Medieval Myth

That men might share
in the divinity of honey,
that they might have wax,
to make the holy
candles for the altar,
God has made the bee,
and graced her
with the spirit of the martyr:
she may sting once only,
in defense of holiness,
and when she does,
she dies.

But the Devil made the hornet,
and the hornet
keeps no sweetness
and no holiness,
and she may sting
as often as the Devil says,
in perpetuity.
All she offers men
is paper and adversity and pain.
As if the hornet
at the Devil's sly behest
intended poetry.

Evening Prayer

Shutting at day's end his eyes,
a young-enough child
knows already
what for the sake of duty
all the half-believers in his house
will tell him: something
in his world is holy.
Doesn't have a name to give it,
only knows a minute
that his world (because he
and a million-million
other wonders live in it)
is magical beyond imagining.

Soul Fish

All of us together
one last Sunday with the man
who used to make
for us kids out of sunfish
Sundays in the summer;
first you had to catch God's eye:
first you had to take
the living in your hands,
and thread it
on the metal, then commit the line.
Today it is the old man
(showing us the way again)
dangling in the eye of God,
the shadows circling round him
til there's nothing
any of us knows to do
but gather up what
minutes we can find of him
to summerlight.

And Life Everlasting

On the brink of the departure
looms a trickster,
scattering across the year
cocoons that wings
have parted from,
letting men and women dream
of rising to fulfillment
on the wings of everafter.
Animating them
to weave around them
in the autumn light
a dream of April,
teaching them to let their dying
dangle off a limb,
to let their dreaming
hang cocoonlike
off the end of time.

The Roman Officer's Story

What a soldier believes
is his own damn
business, as long as
he isn't stupid about it,
as long as he's got respect for
the gods and the emperor.
Now take Sebastian:
I liked the kid, I really did.
But he got caught
spreading that Christian crap
among the troops.
Really seditious stuff.
What the hell could we do?
If he got stuck full of arrows
and left for dead
who the hell is to blame?
But a funny thing happened.
Some woman (a widow I hear)
took him home with her,
cleaned him up and put some
stuff on his wounds,
and he came around.
And she stayed with him
(for all the good it did her)
til he told her his plan
to come back to the war.
"You're gonna do what?"
she says: "You dumb sonofabitch,
you can't do that."
But sure as hell, he

shows up a week or two later
right here in my tent.
Like I said, I liked the kid.
Thought he was none too bright,
but I liked him.
Wanted to give him
every chance. I asked him,
"You gonna promise
not to spread that Christian
stuff again?" "No sir,
I am a Christian," he says,
"I can't promise that."
So I tried a different tack:
"You gonna burn a little
incense here
to the gods and the emperor?"
"No sir," he says,
"I can't do that, either."
"Then what the hell
did you come back for?"
With a straight face he says,
"Because I'm a soldier, sir."
I could feel myself losing it.
I damn-near had him
clubbed to death right
then and there.
But I got hold of myself.
I wanted, like I said,
to give him every chance.
"You know what I think?"
I says. "I think you
came back to finish dying.

You're all screwed up.
What you need is a good
piece of ass," I says.
"Go get yourself some
wine and a woman.
Come back here
in the morning and answer
my questions then ."
But when he came back,
he stuck to his story.
I hadda have somebody
take the kid out in the yard
and give him what he wanted.
Some Christian woman
took him away and buried him.
Probably plucked out
a lock of his hair.
The Christians are big on
that sort of thing,
or caught a few stains
of his blood on a rag.
Somebody probably got
his uniform, and maybe
a bone or a toenail or two.
I hear a lot of that
stuff is still on display
in a little museum
on the Appian Way.

L.G. Mason

Et Ne Nos Inducas in Tentationem

She knew how beautiful she was.
She knew no boy
could keep his eyes off her.
Once she let one boy come near
and learned that neither she
nor he was to be trusted
with her beauty.
So one morning, overpowered
with the love of God
(or so her legend says)
she rinsed with lime
temptation off her face,
she cleaned perfection
off her for the love of God
and her immortal soul.
There were those who told of her
a different story:
that it was her lover
made a saint of her,
that it was her lover threw
the stuff on her,
when he caught her
with another boy.
We will never know the truth of it.
And yet in later years she wore
(in imitation of the crown
of Christ) a silver circlet
on her head,

studded with sharp
spikelets pointed inward:
a saint by then,
whether it was faith or
penance made her one.
At thirty-one, she lay already
in the unforgiving earth,
unloved by anyone
but God.

Love Stories

Salt Lake City

We two together
watched (on NBC)
the couples of the Wintergames.
Feeling with them every
leap and spin and throw,
sharing in each little slip
and each recovery.
Some dancers know,
you see it in their
glances at each other,
all that matters
is the way together,
not the numbers and the colors
parceled out by
judges of the games.
We two together watching
knew the dance,
even if we lacked the grace,
even if what judges us
allots no medals,
has no numbers to confer
except the years
of our performance
written, first for one,
and then the other,
on a stone.

Angel

You were one of the dying old men
who belonged to
this flirt of a nurse's aid.
She stealing you from the wife
who stood by your side,
to whom you had always been truer
than any man ever had been
to a woman.
And there you were
as your mind flew apart
and your dreams were the dreams
of every old fool.
And there you were
confessing out loud
your schemes
of a fling with a candystriper,
right there in front of the only
woman who loved you.

Young candy tonight
would (climbing up into your sleep)
shed her stripe.
She would laugh as
her long dark hair like flame
draped over your bed,
all her little white
exquisite body blossoming
as she rocked over you.
Until the wonderful skin of her

started to wrinkle,
until, like her uniform,
skin and sinew were peeling away,
leaving, in rhythm over you,
only the gleaming
of naked bone.
And lost and alone,
you would fall into waking.
A waking so deep,
a falling so final that nothing,
not even dreaming,
could rescue you then.

Wild Goose Moment

By the water red with sunset,
by the surface lately
ransomed from a season
turned to stone,
they two together on the shore,
stepping to the one beat,
gesturing together,
consenting to whatever's next.
All the choosing
and the flirting and the fighting
are behind them.
And the rest,
the building and begetting,
the tending to the young,
the gathering and the defending,
are not yet begun.
They dancing
in the moment of reprise,
the moment of the two consenting,
the belonging each to each
and each to everything.

Alone in the Night

She getting in at two am, undressing,
kneeling naked by the bed.
To kneel there is a comfort.
Her husband (on a drunken holiday
himself somewhere)
knows as well as God does
what she's up to,
and he does not care.
Her lover thinks of her on weekends.
Her mate as far as she knows
never thinks of her at all.
And God is just another male
who though he still
wants something from her
never speaks to her.
She kneels a minute before sleeping.
But she does not pray.

Dionysus

Semele, drunken with danger,
met God in the night
as a woman meets a man.
And opening to him,
Semele, for one radiant moment,
was God's only woman.
Once he had touched her
(so lovely was Semele)
not even God
could turn away,
though his passion was more
than she knew how to bear.
She cried out in rapture,
she cried out in pain.
He lifted their son
out of the ruin of her
into himself. The seed,
made real in a woman,
grew in the very womb of God,
where no one
can grow and be sane.
The son of God and Semele,
part human and part divine,
was born the patron of
all such madness
as resurrection and wine.
And longing. And love.

The women flew to him.
Even the women who
longed to be
true to their men.
Waking one twilight,
drunken with wine
they had never
put to their lips,
the vine overgrowing them,
ivy woven over
their looms and their limbs.
Songs of invisible flutes
caressed them,
the beat of a harrowing drum
unbound their
hearts and their hands,
and undid their minds.
They threw open their doors,
they followed
wherever their crazy lord
bade them to come.

What lady who ever drew breath
could say no
to a crazy good-looking kid
driving a chariot
stolen from death?

Cardiac

There is a ruin
in an old man's breast
still hooked up to
(if nothing else) a dream,
still called, for want
of any better name,
a heart. There is a woman
whom an old man
loves as always,
but no longer for the way
the shape of her
undoes him.
Knowing who she is
not by his senses any more,
but by the very beating
of their way together
toward a country where
no rhythm
breaks the calm.

The Orb-weaver's Lover

There is no reason for a song
except to get a lady crazy.
Ask the troubadour
at edges of the orb,
plucking it as if it were a lyre.
Irrepressible romantic
playing (on the threshold
of his love and death)
a serenade that never
rises off the web
into the air. A ballad
no one but his love can hear.

To a Moth-orchid

Out of nothing but orchidness,
sculpture a sorcery
at your center:
a figure the scent and the color,
the shape and the size
of somebody's lover.
Orchid, enchantress, beguiler,
make of somebody
no more a fool than all lovers are.

Lovesong

In the middle of the night,
she wide awake beside him,
sleepless, hurting.
And he turning to her
as he did when they were young.
He whispering,
he laying gentle fingers on her
til her steady breathing
sings to him
the rhythm of the solace
he can give her
even now. Hands of his,
that used to bring
a madder tempo to her body
still can offer her
a little calm, a little respite
when the pain
won't let her be,
in the middle of the night.

Lucky in Love

And the chase
is not to the gifted,
the run
is not to the ready,
the prize
is not to the good.

And the race
is not to the swift
nor the wise,
but only
(God help the race)
to the young.

Consecration of the House

The Angel on the Doorsill

On the very
last day of February,
two thousand and three,
in upstate New York, a country
still covered in
two feet of snow,
he appeared right beneath
the house number:
wings like a suit of new
hope folded tastefully
over the trim shape of him.
Delivering,
to the two old people
who live here,
the news of the spring,
after a winter
more tortured with snowfall
and nights below zero
than anyone
even in Albany could recall.
Blessed are they who persevere
through another February.
Blessed is he
who comes in the name
of the year.

Until Showtime

As good a refuge in winter,
our house,
as any hole in a rock,
as any niche in the cold
where the wings of the dancer
in autumn fold,
to open again when they can.
In April the players, stumbling
out of a closet, scrambling
out of a pot full
of the brightening
bulbs of the spring, linger
backstage at a window,
or wait at a door
for their cue. Nobody
knows how to build
a house that the dancers
of Autumn and April
cannot dedicate
to the year.

The Privateer

No sooner was she
heavy with treasure,
the oak in a yard in the city,
than from above her,
the shadow of sails exploded
over her bough.
The four-master wing
put her lads aboard.
They climbed the rigging,
they seized the booty.
With colors
one more time unfurled,
they put out to see
what more of the city
they could reclaim
for the world.

L.G. Mason

Fruitflies

Home from a week's holiday
in the summer,
you're greeted, the minute
you come in the door,
by the scent of the overripe
in the kitchen,
there in the cabinet
under the sink.
You open it,
and a havoc of infinitesimal
craft are airborne.
Spilling into the dining room,
invading the parlor,
taking every sill
and panel and window.
Turn your back
for a week on the world
and the world is itself again,
discovering
the unguarded fortress,
the careful illusion
your dwelling is,
and sending the troops in,
to make of your house
a little of what the world
has always been.

Museum Piece

Diving in among the dead,
discover there
the untransfigured,
each suspended on a pin.
Deliver, furtive beetle,
all the spirits of the still,
conferring on the lost
a trinity of worm
and wing and waiting,
empowering your young
to bring the fallen
home into the year.

L.G. Mason

Sapsuckers

One springtime in the Helderbergs,
the morning-drummers
found the metal boxes
hung up in the sky
by the people of Verizon.
Ticki-tik-ti-dik-dik-tik,
the metal sang from dawn to noon.
Once a drummer tried one,
or heard a rival trying one,
he never went back to wood
to tell a lady-feather who he was.
Wood was good to tap, to take
whatever else you needed,
but to let a lady know
how valiantly your bill
could meet the morning,
there was nothing better
than to make the metal
ring across the country,
rattle with your prowess,
with your promise
of the good days dawning.

Written

Scattered over the monitor
at four in the morning,
shapes no bigger than letters:
y-moths and t-hoppers,
flies the size
of the dots on the i's.
Swarming and circling
to find one another.
Real as the summer,
dancing amid the seasonless
clutter of words,
to the rhythm
the world will still live on
when letters are gone.

Consecration of the House

Out of the washbasin,
over the tile terrain,
wings embracing
a house as their country.
River enough
in the plumbing
to nurture their young.
Season enough
in the windowgleam
for courting, mating,
committing
their seed to the stream.

Each Other We Have Not Always

The Fever

The plague in Albany began,
one quiet day
in nineteen hundred four,
to burn his daughters up:
they started one by one
the throwing-up and breaking out
in color; one by one they
died in front of him,
and after each calamity
he cried out to the Lord,
"Let that be an end to it!"
And every time, God's answer
was another little girl
catching fire.
Finally his woman, leaning
hour after hour over
first one dying daughter
then another,
caught God's eye,
and caught the fever,
then with a weariness
nobody'd ever seen in her
caught the next deliverance
to elsewhere.
"All my girls are gone,"
the man lamented,
whisky glass in hand, day in,
day out, hour after hour.

Of his family only he
and one boy (indestructible,
cantankerous) remained.
Not enough family,
not after this,
to bring the fruits of
a troubled day home to,
to turn a man back
out of a terminal mercy,
the whisky (in which he drowned).
Meanwhile the kid, abandoned,
learned a trade:
the kid was talented.
Grown up,
he could lay a fancy brick
like nobody in Albany,
and play the banjo
like a fallen angel.
And he found a lovely lady
(happily the young forget)
and sired three feisty,
clever, lovely, vulnerable
daughters of his own.

*****

And one of his daughters
who never married
died young.
And one, who married
a solid, stolid
postmaster-plumber,

bore him four girls.
But one of the banjoman's daughters
who played the piano
and did what she pleased
and didn't mind testing the banjoman,
fell in love with a drummer.
Plenty of folks gave her warning,
not least among them
her father:
drummers are crazy,
drummers are no damn good.
Would she listen?
When she grew great
with the beat of the drummer,
when she grew round
with a daughter,
well, the banjoman
saw to it even a drummer
did what was right.
And she married the drummer.
And he loved her as much as
a drummer can,
and a daughter was born to them.
You were born to them, Adrienne,
all of the banjoman's
song in your heart,
all of the drummer's
merciless beat in your blood.
And lord, how you sang.
You would have sung
every heroine's joy
and every heroine's sorrow

from here to forever,
except no tune was ever
a match for the rhythm.
You threw your talent away
on a low-life shallow
good-looking ne'er-do-well
one step ahead of the law,
and ran away with him,
far away from the song.

And he stayed out of jail
long enough to give you
a son and a daughter,
in between his bouts with
his other women,
one of whom
he deserted you for.
And left you alone,
to put the music together again.

And when you remarried,
(lord, you could pick 'em)
it was an alcoholic,
self-centered, epileptic,
poetry-blathering academician.
But you and he in your own
peculiar ridiculous manner
loved each other.
And lived together
in this house and that one
for many a year.

Beethoven

One of the doctors
kept a new-born son
out of your arms. Everyone knew
he was going to die,
why torture you with him?
And one of the doctors saved him:
working heroic and feverish,
and only god knew how wise,
restored him (an undersize
screaming calamity)
to the world: crippled in
this limb and that one,
lacking the hearing in one ear,
the sight in one eye;
and all the hours
you and he had spent apart
were lost forever.
But you brought him home,
and through the years,
you gave him
what he could be given, even
something of the magic
of the old piano in your house.
Starting at a time when he was
scarcely old enough to sit,
you put him down
on the piano-bench,
you took his stricken

hands in yours
on journeys up the scale and down,
unclenched each palsied finger,
pressed it tight
against each key.

You listened as he,
growing up,
was lured to the piano.
You smiled at something haunting,
some half-recollection
of the soft
sonata-shapen moonlight
that had drifted
off your fingers over him
as he lay dreaming, long ago.

The Hostess

Up at the lake,
you welcomed them all,
every cousin and possum
and muskrat and aunt,
every heron and grandson
and old friend from school,
every wild goose
and stray cat.
A ballet of sunfish
would play at your feet
off the end of the dock
in the red afternoon,
you choreographing
with toes and crackers the dance.
At morning,
you, out in the lake for a swim,
surrounded by pickerel
or by bass. And once,
while you swam,
no less a bird than an eagle
discovered you.
Young one, unwhited,
unwise in the ways
of the shapes at the surface,
soaring a minute,
then hurtling at you.
You showed him
enough of a splash
to bear witness:
you were no little fish.

Barely in time,
the eagle, awake
to the scope of his prey,
checked his fall,
veered away, as you
cataloged in your heart
the shape of the talon,
a fine signature
for your registry
of the great and the small
who visited you at the lake.

The Weeding

You longed
to get into your garden
one more time before the snow,
to rid it of the incorrect
and the irrelevant.
Instead you lay tormented
with an episode of your rebelling body
in the last fine weather of the fall.
Soon enough the white
would cover everything.
You'd have to start again in spring
from the beginning.
Still, you had to get it right.
I knew, laboring indoors
to clear away the verbal plantain
from these lines.
Not that anybody-much will ever see
what either one of us has grown.
And yet a garden is a garden.
There is only so much time
to get it done.

L.G. Mason

Encore

Redemption of the winter
in the house where
you and I grew old together
was the grand piano
in the living room.
Not since you were young
had you spent so many
hours at a keyboard.
They returned to your piano,
all your favorites,
like old lovers:
Debussy, a furtive smile
across your morning,
Chopin dancing with you
in the afternoon,
before Rachmaninoff
seduced your twilight hours.
"Does it bother you?"
you asked me.
And I said, "I love it," and I did,
too old, too full of you
for jealousy.

Seizing the Fantastic Night

Our neighbors
(older folks than even you and I)
secured their property
with light that (turning on
in answer to a shadow)
flooded down upon
a burglar in the night,
or on a passing possum,
deer, or mouse.
One night the lights went
totally berserk
and started flashing off and on.
At first we tried to sleep,
but it was hopeless,
even with the shades drawn,
and we had to call them up
at twenty minutes before midnight.
Our neighbor, waking,
took me for a prankster.
"You have the wrong number,"
he said, and hung up.
But when I called again,
he came around.
He fiddled for the better part of an hour
with the fool contraption,
to turn it off.
We lay together meanwhile,
you and I,

still caught in the apocalypse
of merciless and endless
flashing light.
Still totally awake together.
And you had a headache
which I tried to soothe
with kisses and the touch of a hand.
And one thing led to
one more gentle thing.
And two old people lay together
closer and then closer.
Two old people
naked in the flashing neighborlight
fumbling over one another
in a garish, luminous,
and crazy moment
til at last the darkness
fell across our sheer exhaustion,
and we spilled
into our separate dreams,
having wasted not one minute
of a night late in our
vigil on a chancy planet
when our neighbors' madness
would not let us rest.

The Echo of the Beat

And the drummer man was gone.
The man your Mama loved
or anyway the man
she told the world she loved
when she was young.
Fifty years by then
he'd been with her.
And with a lot of other women.
Wanted what he wanted from a woman.
When he wanted it.
Some nights she told him 'No,'
but he was such a giant of a man,
and she was small.
Some days, as years went by,
she thought she hated him.
Finally, he had
a rumbling in his gut and died,
leaving her alone to pay the bills
and fumble with his tools
to fix a broken this-or-that.
Leaving her alone
to keep the furnace running,
keep the cupboards full,
and keep her body warm at night.
And she began to drift.
He died and everything
began to slip her mind.
He died and (god help her)
it mattered.

Some days she (waking
and forgetting he had gone)
sought him out in every
corner of their house,
and couldn't find him there.
Within a year,
she couldn't find herself there either.
We kept her three years with us,
Finally we took her off to places where
they knew a way to care for her.
Or said they did.
She was never close enough
to anyone again
to hate or love.

Temper One Wound with Another

Cats, and nobody else
in the world,
can quiet the hurting,
undoing your house
the way your diseases undo
the insides of you.
Lacerating a sofa,
shattering porcelain,
cutting into the soil
of a big potted plant.
Only a cat
climbing into your bed,
caressing you
with a row of barbed
blessing, pressing
her face into your face,
can make you forget
a minute or two
the monster
turning inside you.
Some hours of the day,
they rest, the cats.
That's when
the hurt is the worst.
Cherish the craziness.
Soon enough,
not enough cats
will remain in the world
to shut out the pain.

The Brute

Your body
like an ice-sculpture in April.
All the bone in you
(worn thin with your diseases
and your medicine)
breaking up in little pieces,
rattling in pain and prophecy.

I afraid of touching you.
You and I could only
guess at what calamity
my clumsiness
would bring you next.
I appearing too abruptly
in a doorway,
causing you to stir
and jam the fragments of you
into one another,
or I turning in my sleep,
entangling you
in blanket, wrenching you
in agony awake.
Or in the truck
I bumping over pot-holes
or braking
too abruptly at a light.

Wild Roses

I needed your
indictments of me,
as you needed to indict,
lest we both admit
how powerless we were.
I lived in terror
of the day
when I would sin no more.

The Shovel

"No, I don't want you to
dig a damn hole!
If I need a damn hole,
I can dig a damn hole,
now leave me alone."

That's what you told me.
I had it coming.
Watching you pick up a tool
and a pot full of flowers,
I pursued you,
plaguing you with an echo
of some doctor's counsel,
reminding you
things can be done for you.

In spite of the doctors and me,
you began to dig.
But you'd chosen a plot
full of stone,
and got nowhere. Aching,
defeated, you threw
the shovel aside and pointed.
"All right, goddammit,
dig *there*."

And I dug,
and I had no better luck
than you in the shale.
And you wanted to cheer.

Finally I
pulled with my hands
enough of the stones away
to allow you to put
a few roots in the ground,
and cherish them with topsoil
and a little water.
And let them a little while
take what they could
from the earth.

The Seizure

With the dullness closing in,
I heard the ringing
and I found the telephone.
You were at the hospital.
Why had I not picked you up?
I tried to tell you and I failed.
But could I drive?
Never took the time to wonder.
Only ran out to the truck,
backed it down the driveway
(crazy old man) and took off.
Found the building.
Luckily the route was easy.
Prayed that you'd be
waiting on the ground floor.
No such luck.
You were somewhere in that vastness,
in a room I'd been in
when my mind was whole.
Thought if I got on an elevator,
I'd remember.
Going up without a floor
to give them,
lost amid the called and chosen.
Coming down again,
there were the three of us.
The pilot of the metal vehicle,
and someone in a long black bag,
and me. Every floor
had looked like any other.

Wild Roses

I stumbled through the seven levels
of St. Peters, Albany,
down any random corridor,
peering into this room, that one
for (I guess) an hour.
Then, the nightmare clearing,
this world drifting
piecemeal back to me,
I rode the elevator
one more time, to four,
and asked somebody
the way to "Infusion,"
finally the word was there.
Somebody brought me to you.
"I could have come home
in a cab, for Christ's sake" you said.
Picturing me laid out
on a pavement somewhere.
All the way home,
two old people
railing at each other,
and I thought of
how chaotic it will be
in the looming hour
when one of us, longing for
the other, looking for the other,
needs to learn
the way out of the bewilderment
alone.

L.G. Mason

December Twenty-something

You came downstairs this morning
and the sky had fallen.
And the tree
had slipped out of its mooring.
Little half-suns, quarter moons,
and delicatest glass star-scatter
littering the floor.

Little broken icicles
and cats and lutes and g-clefs,
little strawberries and apples
and two jagged halves
of one spectacular glass figure
who'd presided at the tip.
All the pieces of your memory,
the bits of every Christmas
fussed over every year for days.
If only I had
put the base together right.
I strained to put
the earth and heaven back in place.
You cried out, "Stop it!
More are falling, more are breaking!"

You rescued what you could,
but couldn't bear
to put it all at risk again.
There would be no tree
this Christmas, you declared.
But after we had lifted
all the years back into place,
and swept the rubble off the floor,
we found your memory,
enough of it to fill the tree,
to risk it in the season
one year more.

Requiem

One winter solstice eve,
they telephoned you
from the home.
Your mama had the virus,
nothing could be done.
And all night long,
you held your mama's hand,
looking into the eyes of her
narrowing already
to meet the dark.
She reaching her face
up into the mask,
her breath fogging the plastic.
Her mouth gaping open
into a last ellipse
hardening into place
on her face
as she, smaller
than anybody remembered,
metamorphosed into a skin
for the world to cast.
Nothing to do but abide by
what little you knew
of what she'd have wanted.
Letting them
burn her to cinders.
Taking her home in an urn,
the one she'd have chosen.

The Snow in Albany

Winter of two thousand three:
thirty inches.
In a few days, thirty more.
And in between,
the layering of ice
to steal away the spirit
of the pines, the bending
and the give of them.
Then the weight and the wind
on the pine branches,
playing on the asymmetries
wrought by the sun
and the power-company.
Great trees leaning,
coated in glass
under the weight of the snow.
Finally pines uprooted,
one and then another
crashing down about us,
two of them narrowly
missing the house,
taking the power lines down.

The lines and the trees
were like that all over town.
It was days
before lights were back on,
and the houses warm.

We stayed the first night
(should have known better)
and made a fire.
The birchwood
was too freshly cut.
It made a slow and smoky flame.
And we ran out of kindling.

We gathered up the cats
and a little food
and a few changes of clothes,
and we made our escape.
Once that week,
you cried a long time in my arms.
Your mother gone.
The trees you cherished lost,
your house turned cold and dark.
In a few days, we came home
to a January colder
than anyone could remember,
even in Albany.
It was a winter worth surviving.

Poems We Have Always With Us

I do not love you enough
(last night you told me again)
now that I'm old.
I do not listen.
I go into a little room
and I write my silly verses,
hours at a time,
and leave you alone.
You'd hardly know I was here.
I'm not the thoughtful
man you married.
So you tell me,
recalling the passionate
drunken young fool
who used to pursue you.
Not as good at wanting
or at being wanted
(you and I)
as once we were.
This morning,
I lay near your hurting,
haunted by
images out of my dream.
I wanted to sing them,
to slip out of bed
and commit them to paper.
But turning to me
in your sleep, you moaned
and I kissed you
and put my hand to your face

and I stayed by your side,
and bathed you in
vanishing moments,
in images
spilling over the dawn
like precious oil.
A foolish voice
in the back of my mind
reminded me images
might have been turned
to poems
and given to memory.
I lay by your side,
only half-aware
that one of these mornings,
one of us will wake
beside the other's shadow.
One of us will know
whether we were loved enough.

The Silences God Sings While Fishes Dance

Wild Roses

Out walking, lady,
on the verge of April,
at the brink of eighty
and the edges of your property,
you blundered on their lair.
What was this that lightly
hugged your ankles,
tugged (at first benignly
then more tightly)
at your clothes?
You looking down, discovering
the dragon-arches,
supple serpent bodies,
branches of the rose
alive with spines.
You imprisoned
in preposterous clutches,
laughed and lifted
branches off you. But the smile
spilled off your eyes
as this one and then that one
rediscovered you,
tendriling your arm, your shoulder,
reaching round your waist,
attaching to your thighs.
Here and there
where thorns intruded,
droplets, oozing scarlet through
your shallow surfaces,
escorted you to vertigo.

You dreaming of the eerie
whisper of the earth.

Neighborlady
leaning over you,
unraveling the nightmare,
took you by the hand,
led you to a house,
brewed tea.
You gazed a long while afterward
out kitchen windows
at the stems-undragoned
that were after all
nothing but wild roses.
Nothing in the world
was altered except you,
summoned to the brink of eighty,
shown the earth,
and whispered-to.

Coyotes

Last night a silver sliver
of a blade
cut through the dark.
In the light of waning,
carried on the wind
across the lake,
the howling of the elders
and the yipping of the young,
about the shrill confession
of a dying thing.
Coyotes sang to heaven,
while an edge
in the clutches of God
cut the throat of the sky.

L.G. Mason

A Dream Knows More Than a Man Does

Awake at the brink
of elderly dawn,
reaching back into the night
for the dream,
the one I remember
by no particular
imagery, only the fear.
Reaching back into the center,
beyond the façade
of the way into morning,
beyond the mirage
of the waking and waking,
beyond the self
with a role and a name.
Between this illusion
and that one,
I dream,
remembering what I dare.

Alzheimer Heroine

Cinderellable
any night again or any
moment of the day,
dressable in glitter
and forgivable a minute
all the years
and all her pain,
turning into anyone
she's ever been:
child in her father's house,
unwidowed wife,
young girl, until
God-knows-what-midnight
drops her off again
in a forsaken
corner of her waking.
Lately (thank god anyway
for that) she never
wakes for long.

The Lecher in Pre-op

She standing nude,
indifferent as an artist's model
there among the hospital partitions
that exclude nobody's eyes.
She, whose modesty will soon be
violated by the cameras
leering halfway up her,
not much caring right now
that an old man like myself
can see the outside of her.
She is not beautiful, she is not young.
I've no excuse for
looking at her this long.
(A husband by her side
would like to murder me.)
I've no excuse
except the hurrying forgottenward
of bodies and these eyes.

Midnight Mass

For one of them
it is prayer,
the sign of the cross
they make at the bell
in their corners.
Not for the untested,
unbeaten kid,
hammers for hands,
career on the rise,
death and a smile
in his eyes.
The old journeyman,
his opponent,
ducking a hook,
taking an uppercut,
recognizes the sacrifice,
knows the faithful
(as soon as the kid starts
putting his
punches together)
will be on their feet,
stalking the chosen-of-God
in their hearts.

L.G. Mason

Live at the Village Vanguard One More Time

At the furious piano,
on the frantic drums and bass,
disciples
stirring all the faithful
into frenzy: making straight
and clamorous and wild
his way. Laying into place
a torrid beat,
a promise of salvation
like a beam of light
focused in the smoke
of cigarette and maryjane.
He at last is come, the man,
to lay sweet suffering,
a love supreme,
a straight soprano sax
across the beam.
To touch the pearled keys
like prayerbeads,
breathe the praises
through a horn.
A spear-in-the-side melody
invites you home:
come fight the good fight,
die with him.

A Dream of Homecoming

No traditional game
this year in the stadium.
Down on the field no children
breaking themselves
across one another.
No marching bands.
Only (up in the stands)
a babble of foolish old
women and men,
our poetry in our hands,
all reading at once.
Time like beetles,
hollowing out the bleachers
beneath us,
bringing to pass
the ludicrous earthward parade
of the crumbling wood
and shattering bone.
Nobody cheering
as words running through us
cover the final yards
home.

L.G. Mason

In November

Branches
at the margins of the aspen
are still flying yellowed banners
round a year the cold
has hollowed out.
When the wind in half light rises,
it's as if survivors
(just a handful of them)
are determined to hold
something for the summer,
bearing colors
that are not a summer's colors,
rattling a rust of arms
in a defeated cause.
When the wind dies,
so does the illusion.
So do cause and its betrayal
and the quarrel
between aspens and the cold.
Nobody
unless it is a man
makes war on any season
of his own.

Epilogue

One eerie night
near the total eclipse of me,
something that still had a name
burst out of my body
on spindly legs and dwelt
under a muted moon
in the gossamer ruin of a dream.
And lay in wait
for whatever small wing
(wanting, discovering,
nearly believing
whatever little it can)
still surfaces in an old man.

The Driving Home

They burst half-recognized
out of the dark,
the names of the roads
in the rain
on a moonless night.
How can you be lost
here among these signs
off-and-on-electric
in the lightning,
here among these turnings
that a moon ago you knew
if you knew anything.
How can you be true
to who you are
until you give up
every name,
til you pretend no more
that any route to anywhere
belongs to you?

For Linda

One January evening
in your fifty-seventh winter,
all the family
came falling round you
like the snow. You alone now
in the house your mother left you.
Both kids married now,
Mike gone.
And the snow kept coming.
Half a foot so far.
Another foot by morning,
someone on the television said.
And the phone kept ringing.
Started about six,
your cousin Karen's voice:
Nancy's husband Lennie
died this morning,
cancer (you had known he had it)
blossoming in merciless detail
in Karen's version,
putting fingers of perdition
into now this organ
of poor Lennie and now that one.
Then Karen hung up,
called away by
something her grandson was doing,
and left you to your television.

In an hour again the phone.
News of Uncle Jack in hospice.

Probably he wouldn't
last the weekend.
(How could that be?
You had seen him just a month ago.
He had looked great.
He was on his way to Florida
with what's-her-name,
his girlfriend.)

Lennie you had hardly known.
Jack was something else.
Nothing on the television
was enough distraction.
And the phone kept ringing.
There had been an accident.
Nobody killed, thank God.
And did you know that
Karen's baby granddaughter
had got leukemia?

Meanwhile the memory
of every dying in your life
reached out at you.
Mike resurrected
sitting with you by the tube,
distant and incurable again,
hoarse and in his bathrobe,
tethered to the oxygen.
And then your mother.
You had come
almost too late to see her.
"You must be the daughter, finally,"

the nurse had said.
Everybody dying at the same time,
two hundred miles apart.
How could you be everywhere?

All night long,
the dead kept coming in,
the shapes of everyone
you used to know
kept breaking up like pictures
from a station far away,
kept falling round your solitude
like snow.

I, Metamorphosis

I, still photo
of the new moon
in December, still know
what the seasons were,
still remember,
in the images I hang
across the gulf-
of-hardly-anywhere,
what April (when
the moving picture
moved me) sang.